Seed of Adam

A Nativity Play

BY
CHARLES WILLIAMS

Copyright © 2018 Read Books Ltd.
This book is copyright and may not be
reproduced or copied in any way without
the express permission of the publisher in writing

British Library Cataloguing-in-Publication Data
A catalogue record for this book is available from
the British Library

CHARLES WILLIAMS

Charles Walter Stansby Williams was born in London in 1886. He dropped out of University College London in 1904, and was hired by Oxford University Press as a proof-reader, quickly rising to the position of editor. While there, arguably his greatest editorial achievement was the publication of the first major English-language edition of the works of the Danish philosopher Søren Kierkegaard.

Williams began writing in the twenties and went on to publish seven novels. Of these, the best-known are probably *War in Heaven* (1930), *Descent into Hell* (1937), and *All Hallows' Eve* (1945) – all fantasies set in the contemporary world. He also published a vast body of well-received scholarship, including a study of Dante entitled *The Figure of Beatrice* (1944) which remains a standard reference text for academics today, and a highly unconventional history of the church, *Descent of the Dove* (1939). Williams garnered a number of well-known admirers, including T. S. Eliot, W. H. Auden and C. S. Lewis. Towards the end of his life, he gave lectures at Oxford University on John Milton, and received an honorary MA degree. Williams died almost exactly at the close of World War II, aged 58.

A HISTORY OF THE THEATRE

'The Theatre' is a collaborative form of fine art that uses live performers to present the experience of a real or imagined event. The performers may communicate this experience to the audience through combinations of gesture, speech, song, music, and dance, with elements of art, stagecraft and set design used to enhance the physicality, presence and immediacy of the experience. The specific place of the performance is also named by the word 'theatre' – derived from the Ancient Greek word *théatron*, meaning 'a place for viewing', itself from *theáomai*, meaning 'to see', 'watch' or 'observe'.

Modern Western theatre largely derives from ancient Greek drama, from which it borrows technical terminology, classification into genres, and many of its themes, stock characters, and plot elements. The city-state of Athens is where 'theatre' as we know it originated, as part of a broader culture of theatricality and performance in classical Greece that included festivals, religious rituals, politics, law, athletics, music, poetry, weddings, funerals, and symposia. Participation in the city-state's many festivals – and attendance at the City Dionysia as an audience member (or even as a participant in the theatrical productions) in particular, was an important part of citizenship.

The theatre of ancient Greece consisted of three types of drama: tragedy, comedy, and the satyr play (a form of tragicomedy, similar in spirit to the bawdy satire of burlesque). The origins of theatre in ancient Greece, according to Aristotle (384–322 BCE), the first theoretician of theatre, are to be found in the festivals that honoured Dionysus. These performances (the aforementioned City Dionysia) were held in semi-circular auditoria cut into hillsides, capable of seating 10,000–20,000 people. The stage consisted of a dancing floor (orchestra), dressing room and scene-building area (skene). Since the words were the most important part, good acoustics and clear delivery were paramount. The actors (always men) wore masks appropriate to the characters they represented, and each might play several parts.

Athenian tragedy (the oldest surviving form of tragedy) emerged sometime during the sixth century BCE, and flowered during the fifth century BCE – from the end of which it began to spread throughout the Greek world – and continued in popularity until the beginning of the Hellenistic period. Aeschylus, Sophocles, and Euripides were masters of the genre. The other side of the coin – Athenian comedy, is conventionally divided into three periods; 'Old Comedy', 'Middle Comedy', and 'New Comedy'. Old Comedy survives today largely in the form of the eleven surviving plays of Aristophanes, while Middle Comedy is largely lost (preserved only in a few relatively short fragments in authors such as Athenaeus of Naucratis). New Comedy is known primarily from the substantial papyrus fragments of Menander.

Western theatre developed and expanded considerably under the Romans. The theatre of ancient Rome was a thriving and diverse art form, ranging from festival performances of street theatre, nude dancing, and acrobatics, to the staging of Plautus's broadly appealing situation comedies, to the high-style, verbally elaborate tragedies of Seneca. Although Rome had a native tradition of performance, the Hellenization of Roman culture in the third century BCE had a profound and energizing effect on Roman theatre and encouraged the development of Latin literature of the highest quality for the stage. This tradition fed into the modern theatre we know today, and during the renaissance, theatre generally moved away from the poetic drama of the Greeks, and towards a more naturalistic prose style of dialogue. By the nineteenth century and the Industrial Revolution, this trend continued to progress.

In England, theatre was immensely popular, but took a big pause during 1642 and 1660 because of Cromwell's Interregnum. Prior to this, 'English renaissance theatre' was witnessed, with celebrated playwrights such as William Shakespeare, Christopher Marlowe and Ben Jonson. Under Queen Elizabeth, drama was a unified expression as far as social class was concerned, and the Court watched the same plays the commoners saw in the public playhouses. With the development of the private theatres, drama became more oriented towards the tastes and values of an upper-class audience however. By the later part of the reign of Charles I, few new plays were being written for the public theatres, which sustained themselves on the accumulated works of the previous decades. Theatre was now seen as something sinful and the Puritans tried very hard to drive it out of their society. Due to this stagnant period, once Charles II came back to the throne in 1660, theatre (among other arts) exploded with influences from France, and the wider continent.

The eighteenth century saw the widespread introduction of women to the stage – a development previously unthinkable. These women were looked at as celebrities (also a newer concept, thanks to ideas on individualism that were beginning to be born in Renaissance Humanism) but on the other hand, it was still very new and revolutionary. Comedies were full of the young and very much in vogue, with the storyline following their love lives: commonly a young roguish hero professing his love to the chaste and free minded heroine near the end of the play, much like Sheridan's *The School for Scandal*. Many of the comedies were fashioned after the French tradition, mainly Molière (the great comedic playwright), again harking back to the French influence of the King and his court after their exile.

After this point, there was an explosion of theatrical styles. Throughout the nineteenth century, the popular theatrical forms of Romanticism, melodrama, Victorian burlesque and the well-made plays of Scribe and Sardou gave way to the problem plays of Naturalism and Realism; the farces of Feydeau; Wagner's operatic *Gesamtkunstwerk*; musical theatre (including Gilbert and Sullivan's operas); F. C. Burnand's, W. S. Gilbert's and Wilde's drawing-room comedies; Symbolism; proto-Expressionism in the late works of August Strindberg and Henrik Ibsen; and Edwardian musical comedy. The list continues! These trends continued through the twentieth century in the realism of Stanislavski and Lee Strasberg, the political theatre of Erwin Piscator and Bertolt Brecht, the so-called Theatre of the Absurd of Samuel Beckett and Eugène Ionesco, and the rise of American and British musicals.

Theatre itself has an incredibly long history, and despite the massive proliferation of theatrical styles and mediums – it essentially owes its existence to the ancient Greeks and the Romans. The three main genres; tragedy, comedy and satyre, continue to influence plot themes, directing, writing and acting, with frequent and fascinating interrelations and overlaps. As a genre, it remains as popular today as it has ever been, and continues as a massive influence on popular culture more broadly. It is hoped that the current reader enjoys this book on the subject.

CHARACTERS

THE TSAR OF CAUCASIA (*King of Gold*)

HIS CHORUS

THE SULTAN OF BAGDAD (*King of Frankincense*)

HIS CHORUS

ADAM

EVE

JOSEPH

MARY

THE ARCHANGEL

TWO ROMAN SOLDIERS

THE THIRD KING (*King of Myrrh*), a Negro

MOTHER MYRRH (*Hell*), a Negress

The scene is before the house of Adam; to the right of it are the stables; on the left, at the front, the stump of a tree or a high stone

NOTE

THE only existing manuscript is that of the first version, printed in *Christendom*, September 1937. Of the second version, slightly expanded from the first, there are many typescripts which vary in accuracy, but after some difficulty I have identified the one which contains the author's own faint corrections. This is reproduced here, except that (*a*) the literal corrections necessary to all the scripts have been made; (*b*) two stage directions, added by the producer but approved by the author in performance, have been included on p. 9; and (*c*) the capitalization has been altered in one or two places to conform with the style of the other plays. The list of characters is compiled from the programmes used at the Brentwood and Oxford performances (1937 and 1939), both of which were approved by the author. It seemed best to combine the two, since I was uncertain which would have had his final approval. I should add, that in performance one alteration was required by the Censor.

RAYMOND HUNT

SEED OF ADAM

The TSAR *enters with some of the* CHORUS

CERTAIN VOICES. Juggle, sir; throw up the golden slivers.
OTHER VOICES. Sir, no; show rather the rivers,
  molten and golden streams; fertilizing, barricading,
  cities and nations, from stations of earth-edging Esquimaux
  to the hanging gardens of tropical sense:
  and there the high ships sailing, the deep ships unlading.
FIRST VOICES. Necklaces, bracelets, ear-rings; gaudies and gewgaws!
OTHER VOICES. Purse rather and pocket of outer commerce; mind
  finding after kind, and all traffic its own.
THE TSAR. I am Gaspar,[1] Tsar of Caucasia;
  I sprang from our father Adam's loins
  in a bright emission of coins; Eve's need
  of gilded adornment nourished me to dig and dive.
  Pearls I brought up; springs I let forth: who
  will be beautiful now? who profitable then?
  Men thrive and I take my fee.
  Tricked out in riches half the world follow me;
  who fall, crawl or are kicked into dry ditches.
        [*The* SULTAN *enters, with the rest of the* CHORUS
CERTAIN VOICES. Sir, play; throw up the notes of gold,
  or stir into silver smoke the rich incense.
OTHER VOICES. Sir, no; our old throats are tired.
  Show rather the philosophical plan,
  chess-playing, brick-laying, sooth-saying;
  the design of line, point, and curve.
FIRST VOICES. Titillate the brain by ear and eye!
OTHER VOICES. Build the austere academies to show why.

---

[1] Traditionally, Melchior is the King whose gift is gold. C. W. has reversed Melchior and Gaspar, here and in an early poem. [*Ed.*]

SEED OF ADAM

THE SULTAN. I am Melchior, Sultan of Bagdad.
Adam my father and Eve my mother
construed me aloof from sister and brother
through a post-paradisal afternoon.
I build my mosques under a philosophical moon;
I ride on the body's curves through spirals of air
to the bare and rare domes of Bagdad my see.
I give to whoever serves with me
gnomic patterns of diagrammatic thrills.
Half the world live in my train;
who refrain, bereft of brain, are left to common ills.
SEMI-CHORUS. Give us the golden matter,
SEMI-CHORUS.   and the golden chatter,
THE CHORUS. for to-morrow everything begins again.
         [*They gather about the* KINGS, *some sitting or lying*
ADAM [*coming out of the house*]. Dullards of darkness, light's lazy-
    bones,
poor primitives of our natural bareness,
where's your awareness? will moans and groans
for gold of brawn or brain regain
the way to the entry of Paradise? up!
shut your eyes, will you? or make a play
for your leisure, and a treasure of your idleness? You,
have you nothing better to do
in our world but play hide and seek with oblivion?
Say, say something, say
who are you? I will tell you, tell you what you knew,
I am Adam.
SEMI-CHORUS. Father Adam, the pasture is thin,
the sheep and the hogs are thin, our coats
button thinly about our throats
thrawn with wind and thirsty for wine.
Exchanges—his and mine—help us
to bear with the bitterness of having nothing.

What should *we* do, feeling for Paradise?
Better to suck at the heel of the Tsar.
SEMI-CHORUS. Father Adam, if we go looking and snooping round corners,
we see terrible shapes trooping,
things eagle-beaked, giants with scimitars.
In Eden you found them friendly; here
what should we do but hide while they stride and deride
the bitterness of our having nothing?
Have you seen us slinking from those neighbourly taunts?
Better to go drinking the rhythms of the Sultan.
ADAM. If you found Paradise, you would find everything.
THE CHORUS. Call with the old bluster to muster by masses, and seek!
SOLO.   Speak civilly, father!
                    Where
shall we go? climb invisible cords into the air?
for road, river, and lane
are searched; it is not to be found.
THE CHORUS. And to-morrow everything begins again!
SOLO. What is this way? behind what sight or sound?
SOLO. He lost it, and he cannot say.
SOLO. There is not any.
SOLO.   Yes; it is bought for a penny
and slept off.
SOLO.   No; wise men have recognized
it is only our mothers' forms rationalized.
SOLO. The Tsar declares it is hope learning to grope.
SOLO. The Sultan says it is sensation living in negation.
SOLO. It is the loss of the one thing prized
masochistically advertized;
SOLO. or adolescence flushed with immature sense.
ADAM. Babies!
THE CHORUS. Who lost it?

SEED OF ADAM

ADAM.   I. What do you know,
children, of what living on this earth is like then?
THE SULTAN. Father, you must not think you are everyone.
THE TSAR. Your children are men and women, and not you.
THE SULTAN. Individualized essence of you, perhaps;
THE TSAR. with each his particular Paradise in a nutshell.
THE SULTAN [*touching his lyre*]. Nuts! nuts!
THE TSAR [*throwing gold pieces*]. Nuts! nuts!
BOTH.   Nuts for the men-monkeys!
Monkey-nuts! follow, follow, monkey-nuts!
scratch and snatch for a portion of monkey-nuts!
grab and grizzle for a ration of monkey-nuts!
houp-la!
> [*The* CHORUS, *chattering and fighting, run about like monkeys. They gradually become involved in a general fierce battle and drift off, following the* KINGS, *with high shrieks*]

ADAM. I must set my law upon them; one thing first.
> [*He turns, meeting* EVE, *who has come out of the house at the noise*]

EVE. Are they fighting again?
ADAM.   What else?
They have not the pain that in us stops us fighting.
EVE. Have they found anything?
ADAM.   Nothing, my Eve.
They cannot find the centre, the core of the fruit
where the root of return is. I dropped it; it is gone.
Where is Mary?
EVE.   Mary has gone to the fair.
ADAM. Under the Mercy! . . . what is she doing there?
EVE. Watching mountebanks, laughing at clowns,
applauding jugglers and tightrope walkers,
listening to talkers, admiring lovers,

riding with children on the roundabout,
everywhere in the middle of the rout,
being, by her nature, all things to all men.
ADAM. Will she never discover any preference? any partial
liking for this where or that when?
Will she never care to marshal phenomena?
Cows, clowns, and crowns are alike to her—
has she not a trick of nursing the sick,
and as agile through all as the honey-plucking bee,
catching as much sweet there as from booths at the fair?
She must follow now another mind than mine.
I am set. Call Joseph; they shall be married.
EVE. Married! Mary? but why? and why Joseph?
ADAM. Lest I should die. She shall be wedded
lest our youngest born should be a prey
in her simplicity to her sisters and brothers.
I will not have her a scullion and a scorn
in the huts of Caucasia or the harems of Bagdad.
Joseph is a warlike and dutiful lad.
Call him.
EVE. What is he, where is he, now?
ADAM. Lieutenant-general of the Sultan's horse,
an Islamite, a genius in cavalry tactics!
To see swung whole squadrons in the charge,
and—in a wild clatter of words breaking—flung
down the speaking of a poem, when the matter is sprung
to the flashing and slashing of a steel line
at the throat's blood. Hafiz taught him
and Omar; he outgenerals them; call him.
EVE. Will Mary have him?
ADAM. As soon as any.
O pest on her for a zany of goodwill!
EVE. Husband!
ADAM. Be easy. I am petulant. My want

worries at my throat, while she wants nothing,
nor ever sighs for nor even denies Paradise.
EVE. Paradise perhaps is hers and here.
ADAM. Among the sick or at the fair?—
Look, there she comes: call Joseph, I say.
He is in Bagdad's train. I must go again
to quieten their brawls. I will give them peace.
I will show them if I am Adam for nothing.

[JOSEPH *and* MARY *enter*

ADAM. Joseph, am I your lord?
JOSEPH. In all things, sir,
under the justice of God.
ADAM. Your father, Mary?
MARY. Sir, by the Direction.
ADAM. It is well; hear me.
I do and undo; I am Adam. Paradise
shuts its last mouth upon us, and I am afraid.
It may be, after I have conquered yonder apes,
and shaped them to placabilities, that I shall find
by counting them some form unguessed,
some archangel disguised, some person or place
where is the grace of the Return. If, well;
if not, the thing this world must soon become
catches us up. Whether this be or not
I am determined you two shall be married.
A heart of purity and a mind of justice
to be integrity. What say you?
JOSEPH. Sir,
I am of no more worth to the princess Mary
than the fly-flick of her mule's tail.
MARY. But as much, Joseph, indeed.
JOSEPH. You hear, my lord?
ADAM. Never mind her.
Since she loves all, she loves you. What of you?

SEED OF ADAM

JOSEPH. She is the manifest measurement of God's glory correcting time.

ADAM [*motioning them before him*]. You are both my best of children.

[JOSEPH *and* MARY *kneel;* ADAM *raises his right arm*]

By the single indecipherable Name
I swear you, Joseph and Mary, to betrothal.

[JOSEPH *and* MARY *rise and face each other. The upraised palms of their right hands touch. They turn to face* ADAM]

When I return from conquering the world, be ready,
as then shall be, in time and space, convenient.
Come, Eve.

[ADAM *and* EVE *go out*]

JOSEPH. Am I appointed for your husband? . . .
Answer, princess . . . no ? no then, do not speak,
do not break through such an outgoing stress of light,
as is the sovereign blessedness of the world,
there indivisible, all ways else divisible.
Do not with descent, O altitude, even of mercy,
sweeten the enhancèd glance of those still eyes
which to my lord's house, and to me the least,
illumine earth with heaven, our only mortal
imagination of eternity,
and the glory of the protonotary Gabriel.

[MARY *stretches out her hand to him; he kneels and kisses it*]

MARY [*murmuring the name*]. Gabriel, Gabriel: well spoken is the name.
As I came from the fair I looked back; there
I saw it all in a sheath and a shape of flame,
having an eagle's head that turned each way
as if it were guarding something and looking for something.
Its eyes burned at me; the noise
of the hurly-burlies and the hurdy-gurdies,
the ball-spinners, the silk-sellers, the rum-peddlers,

the swings, and the songs, rose to a whirring voice,
the air was a hum of sound; I heard it come
as if the fair all rose in the air and flew
on eagle's wings after me; I ran
through the fear and the laughter and the great joys.
I came by the vineyards to my father's roof;
there it held aloof a little.
I saw you; I gave you my hand, Joseph,
at my father's will. It has still power,
this hand of Adam's daughter, on all creatures of heaven.
JOSEPH [*as he kneels*].   O princess,
your hand is the fact of God's compact of light.
MARY. I have heard such talk among the lovers at the fair.
Bless you for telling me, Joseph.
    [*He releases her hand. The* ARCHANGEL *appears at the back, as it were casting sleep towards* JOSEPH, *who sinks slowly forward, and lies still*]
MARY.   Joseph!

[*A pause*

        Joseph!

[*She sees him lying*

THE ANGELIC CHORUS [*without*]. Adonai Elohim! Adonai Elohim![1]
THE ARCHANGEL [*standing behind* MARY]. Adonai hu ha-elohim!
THE CHORUS [*as the angelic army without*]. Shalom lach eschet-chen,
    Adonai immach beruchah at bannashim.
Al-tiri Miryam ki-matsat chen lifne ha-elohim.
Vehinnach harah veyoladt ben vekaret et-shemo Yeshua.
MARY. How shall these things be, seeing I know not a man?
THE CHORUS. Ruach hakkodesh tavo alayieh ugevurat elyon tatsel
    alayich: al ken Kadosh yeamer layyillod ben-ha-elohim.

[1] The Hebrew is written phonetically, as for the Sephardi pronunciation (vowel sounds as in Italian, all *r*'s distinctly sounded, *ch* as in *loch*). The Ashkenazi pronunciation can be used if desired.

SEED OF ADAM

MARY. Behold the handmaid of the Lord; be it unto me
according to thy word.
  [*The* ARCHANGEL *passes round and enters the stables.* MARY
    remains rapt]
JOSEPH [*he rises to his knees, as before, and wakes*]. Under the
  Protection! Mary . . . Mary . . .
MARY.   Yes, Joseph?
JOSEPH. Mary, you are changed; you are in love.
MARY.   Yes, Joseph.
JOSEPH [*starting up*]. Ah, ah! but who . . . ?
MARY.   No one, Joseph.
  Only in love.
JOSEPH.   It must be then with someone.
MARY. Dearest, you did not hear: we said *in love*.
  Why must, how can, one be in love with someone?
JOSEPH. Because . . . but that is what *in love* means;
  one is, and can only be, in love with someone.
MARY. Dearest, to be in love is to be in love,
  no more, no less. Love is only itself,
  everywhere, at all times, and to all objects.
  My soul has magnified that lord; my spirit
  rejoiced in God my saviour; he has regarded
  the nothingness of his handmaid. He has thrust
  into this matter his pattern of bones, as Eve's
  towers of cheeks and arrogant torches of eyes
  edify red earth into a pattern of manhood.
JOSEPH. But it must be at some time and in some place.
MARY. When you look at me, dear Joseph, do you think so?
JOSEPH. Babylonia and Britain are only boroughs of you.
  Your look dimensions the world. I took once
  a northward journey to find fables for the Sultan
  and heard a lad on the hill of Faesulae syllabling
  a girl of Faesulae who nodded good-morning at him,
  and that her form timed the untimed light.

11

Place must be because grace must be,
and you because of glory. O blessing,
the light in you is more than you in the light.
MARY. The glory is eternal, and not I,
and I am only one diagram of the glory:
will you believe in me or in the glory?
JOSEPH. It is the vision of the Mercy.
MARY.   Hold to that.
But for salvation—even of those who believe
that time and place and the one are the whole of love—
Love—O the Mercy! the Protection!—
shall make his flesh as one in time and place.
It shall come in the time of Augustus Caesar,
in the place of Bethlehem of the Holy Ghost,
in the coast of Judaea: not quite Jerusalem,
but not far from Jerusalem, not far but not quite.
O Thou Mercy, is this the secret of Thy might?
When Thou showest Thyself, that Thou art not there
to be found? we find Thee where Thou art not shown.
Thou art flown all ways from Thyself to Thyself,
and Thy ways are our days, and the moment is Thou.
O Thou Mercy, is this the thing to know?
Joseph, come, take me to Bethlehem;
there the apparition and the presence are one,
and Adam's children are one in them;
there is the way of Paradise begun.
    [*They move round the stage to the stone. As they go, the*
    CHORUS *re-enter on all sides*]
THE CHORUS. In Thule, in Britain, in Gaul, in Rome,
among the slim pillars of Bagdad, in round mounds of Caucasia,
we heard the maxim that rules the schools of prophets:
this also is Thou; neither is this Thou.

With double hands and single tongues
the prophets climb the rungs of heaven,

in the might of a maxim gained and given:
this also is Thou; neither is this Thou.

But we who wander outside the rules and schools
compromise and complain,
before the clot in the blood has shot to the heart or brain:
this is not quite Thou and not quite not.

Sister, sister, did you dream?

What did you see on the banks of the body's stream,
in Thule, in Britain, in Gaul, in Rome,
under Bagdad's dome, by the mounds of Caucasia?
SOLO. One came walking over the sand,
one and a shadow from a desert land;
I saw a knife flash in a black hand.

At daybreak a child is born to the woman;
he grows through the noon to his full stature;
she devours him under the moon; then at morn—
THE CHORUS. Save us, Father Adam, or we perish!—
SOLO. or in a mirage of morn the child is reborn.
And to-morrow everything begins again.
THE CHORUS. From bone, from brain, from breasts, from hands,
from the mind's pillars and the body's mounds,
the skies rise and roll in black shadows
inward over the imperial soul:
over our sighs in the moon of dusty sorrow—
O, O, could everything begin before to-morrow;
over the creak of rusty grief—
to-morrow will be soon enough for belief;
over the kitchens of a pot neither cold nor hot,
and the thin broth, and the forming of the clot—
not quite Thou and not quite not.

Father Adam, save us or we perish.

[MARY *sits on the stone,* JOSEPH *stands behind her. From*

opposite sides two ROMAN SOLDIERS *run in, turn to the front, and come to the salute*]
FIRST SOLDIER. Octavianus Caesar Augustus,
SECOND SOLDIER. filius Julii divi Augustus,
BOTH SOLDIERS. orders the world in the orbit of Rome.
FIRST SOLDIER. Oaths and service to the lord Augustus;
SECOND SOLDIER. incense and glory to the god Augustus:
BOTH SOLDIERS. to the god Augustus and the Fortune of Rome.
[*They wheel inwards, and fall back on either side.* ADAM *re-enters as* AUGUSTUS, *accompanied by* EVE *and the two* KINGS]
ADAM. I was Julius, and I am Octavianus,
Augustus, Adam, the first citizen,
the power in the world, from brow to anus,
in commerce of the bones and bowels of men;
sinews' pull, blood's circulation,
Britain to Bagdad. I in brawn and brain
set knot by knot and station by station.
I drive on the morrow all things to begin again.
Look, children, I bring you peace;
I bring you good luck; I am the State; I am Caesar.
Now your wars cease; what will you say?
THE TSAR. Hail, Caesar; I am your occupation for the days.
THE SULTAN. I am your sleeping-draught for the nights: hail, Caesar.
THE CHORUS. Hail, Caesar; we who are about to die salute you!
ADAM. I will take now a census of the whole world,
the nations and generations of the living and dead,
to find whether anywhere it has been said
what place or person Paradise lies behind,
even among the prophets who made a formula for the mind.
Each man shall answer, on or under earth,
from Cain and Abel, who were first to explore
womb and tomb, and all whom women bore,

SEED OF ADAM

to the pack that died at Alexandria yesterday.
Answer, children, and say, if you can. I know
the thing that was threatened comes; there is still time.
Go!
  [*The* SOLDIERS *run out; there is a deep and confused noise.*[1]
  Presently they return, bearing papers]
FIRST SOLDIER. All these millions dead
SECOND SOLDIER.   and dying; these thousands
 dying or dead;
FIRST SOLDIER.   these hundreds, and sixteen—
  [*He drops his spear towards the nearest of the* CHORUS *on his side, who answers as from a sepulchre*]
ONE OF THE CHORUS. and seventeen
ANOTHER.   and eighteen
ANOTHER.   and nineteen
  [*All answer in turn, as the* FIRST SOLDIER, *and then the* SECOND, *pass, pointing their spears. The* SECOND *comes to* JOSEPH]
JOSEPH [*answering according to the number of the* CHORUS]. and thirty-six
           [*The* SOLDIER *points to* MARY
JOSEPH [*answering for her*]. and thirty-seven.
Shall I add one more for the child that slumbers in your womb?

---

[1] The producer suggested that something should be added here, and used to prepare for the entrance of the Third King shortly afterwards. C. W. had begun to write this additional matter, but the following fragment is all that we have:

 TSAR. When the Archangel spoke to you in the true Paradise
  and your heart broke—what did he say, there
  under the trees? something you could not hear
  about not-dying
 SULTAN.   When you ran and pushed
  your way through hedge and river, when you rushed
  down the ledge of rock between the abounding foliage
  near the water rounding Paradise and the world outside—
  a few leaves of the hedge clung to your coats
 TSAR. a few drops of water hung on your skins.
  That was the beginning.
 SULTAN.   Twinning what was one

SEED OF ADAM

MARY. O no, Joseph; he is something different from all numbers;
you cannot tell how or whom. The people are reckoned,
but the child that comes through me
holds infinity in him, and hides in a split second.

[*The* SOLDIERS *return to* ADAM

FIRST SOLDIER. Hail, Caesar; those who are dead
SECOND SOLDIER.   and those about to die
BOTH SOLDIERS. salute you.
Octavianus Caesar Augustus;
filius Julii divi Augustus;
gubernator, imperator, salvator, Augustus.
A VOICE [*off*]. What is this difference between the dying and the
dead?

[*The* THIRD KING *enters, followed by a* NEGRESS, *carrying a scimitar*]

ALL [*except* JOSEPH *and* MARY, *in a general moan*]. Ah!
THIRD KING [*looking round*]. What provincial talk is this? what academic
pedantic dichotomy? O la, brothers!

[*Seeing the* KINGS *left, right*

THE TWO KINGS. Ah, brother, how did you find us?
THIRD KING. Indeed I might not have done;
but my mother here has eyes and a nose,
and with each sun recognized more strongly
gold's glint and censer's smell.
As the wind of infinity blows
earth is always leaving clues for hell,
and hell has only to follow that news of earth.
'*To the* CHORUS]
No wonder you talk so if you have them here
talking of distinctions and differences, smells and savours,
sight of gold, sniff of incense, flavours
of this or that differing degree of corruption.

[*To the* KINGS]
    You left me away in a stony land,
    brothers; I was lonely without you.
    I came to find this mind of Rome,
    this concept, this Augustus, this new Adam.
    Why, father! The old Adam, after all!

ADAM. It is you, is it?

THIRD KING.   I. You saw me
    when you breathlessly slid down the smooth threshold
    of Paradise gate? and saw the things that were hid
    as God warned you you would? did you know
    I was the core of the fruit you ate?
    Did you remember, ungrateful that you are,
    how you threw me away, with such a swing
    I flew over Eden wall, dropped,
    and stuck between two stones?
    You did not see; you did not look after me!
    Smell and taste for you; let the core go to hell.
    But God looks after the sparrows.
    Presently the sun split the core,
    and out grew I, the King of the core.
    I have travelled to get back to you ever since.

EVE. And who is she?

THIRD KING.   Ah, she!
    At the heart of the core, in the core of me,
    lived a small worm you could not see.
    The sun is a generous sun; he set us both free.
    She lives by me, and I by her.
    I call her my little mother Myrrh,
    because of her immortal embalming. We two
    have come, my other mother, to live with you—
    if you can call it living.

ADAM.   What else?

SEED OF ADAM

THIRD KING. O well! She has her own idea of food.
> [*He indicates the scimitar*

The nearer the relation, the better the dish.
But you will not *die*; no, I do not think you will *die*.
I did not, and I have been eaten often,
you may imagine; it was a long way from here,
and a long time ago, that we made our start,
and angels on the way delayed us,
with exhortations of earnest heavenly evangels:
but what can angels do against decaying matter?
Matter can only be corrected by matter,
flesh by flesh; we came through and came on,
and I everlastingly perishing. The worm
of that fruit, father, has a great need to feed
on living form. But I do not think you will die.

ADAM [*to the* SOLDIERS]: Seize her.
> [*They rush forward. She laughs at them, and they fall back on their knees*]

THIRD KING. Whom are you seeking?
Are you come out with swords and staves to take us?
We were often with you in your temples: now—
Father Adam, you were always a fool,
and it seems at the top of your Roman school
no better; will you arrest the itch
with your great hands? will your bands pitch
their javelins against the diabetes of the damned?
The belly is empty in hell though the mouth is crammed:
a monotonous place!

THE CHORUS. Father Adam, lord Augustus!

THIRD KING. Among the stones and locusts she lived on me;
it is your turn—this is my refrigerium.
> [*He draws back. The* TWO KINGS *drop their gold and lute.* EVE *covers her face. The* NEGRESS *walks slowly round, the*

CHORUS *falling on their knees as she passes. At last she comes to* MARY. *Meanwhile the* CHORUS]
THE CHORUS. Call the kings!
 saints! poets!
    prophets! priests!
Call the gospels and the households!
those of Aquino and Assisi!
    Stratford! Chalfont St. Giles!
 caskets of Caucasia!
    censers of Bagdad!
ALL. Help us and save us!
THE TWO KINGS. Balthazar our brother is stronger than we.
THE CHORUS. Call on the households!
    harp-stringer of David!
 hewer of wood for Joseph!
    ink-maker for Virgil!
 galley-captain of Caesar!
    armour-bearer of Taliessin!
ALL. Come to your defences! all heavenly lords,
stand about us with swords.
THIRD KING. Election is made, capital rather than coast:
she thrives most on the dear titbits of perfection.
Sister, you are lovelier than all the rest,
and like the busy blest. She shall eat you alive
for her great hunger; take pity on her appetite.
 [JOSEPH, *drawing his own scimitar, thrusts himself between them*]
JOSEPH [*crying out*]. Ha, ha! to me, my household!
There is no God but God: in the name of God!
 [*The scimitars clash; the* THIRD KING *touches* JOSEPH *in the thigh; he stumbles and is beaten down*]
THIRD KING [*dragging him away*]. Little man, martyrs and confessors
are no good here, nor are poets any good.

SEED OF ADAM

They are all a part of the same venomous blood.
Come away, come away, and wait your turn quietly.
[MARY *takes a step or two forward*
MARY. Dearest, you will find me very indigestible.
The stomach of the everlasting worm
is not omnivorous; it is a poor weak thing:
nor does the fire of Gehenna do more than redden
the pure asbestos of the holy children; if mine,
is for the fire and your dangerous appetite to find.
   [*The* NEGRESS *attacks* MARY *with her scimitar.* MARY *goes back before her, at first slowly, moving round the stage*]
MARY. Sister, how slowly you carve your meat!
THIRD KING. Be easy, sister; you will not get away from us.
MARY. Nor she from me, brother, which is more important.
   [*The movement of the two women quickens and becomes a dance; the scimitar flashing round them in a white fire. The* CHORUS *sway to the movement,* ADAM *only remaining motionless*]
MARY [*suddenly breaking into song*]. Parturition is upon me: blessed be He!
Sing, brothers; sing, sisters; sing, Father Adam.
My soul magnifies the Lord.
THE CHORUS [*hesitatingly*]. My spirit hath rejoiced in God my saviour.
MARY [*dancing and singing*]. For he hath regarded the low estate of his handmaid:
THE CHORUS [*gathering strength*]. behold, from henceforth all generations shall call thee blessed.
   [MARY *at the door of the stable, where the* ARCHANGEL *is seen, catches the uplifted wrist of the* NEGRESS *in her right hand. They stand rigid, foot to foot*]
MARY [*singing joyously through a profound suspense*]. For he that is mighty hath done to me great things;

SEED OF ADAM

THE NEGRESS [*in a shriek of pain and joy*]. and holy is his Name.
  [*She faints at* MARY's *feet*
MARY [*leaning towards* JOSEPH]. Joseph!
My son calls to his foster-father: come!
prince of maidens, hasten to the master of maidenhoods,
and the pillar of maternity.
JOSEPH [*half-rising*].   O mother of the world's brightness,
I sought uprightness, and yet it failed in the end!
MARY. Most dear friend, my lord, it delayed the scimitar
but till my son took flesh under its flash:
the heavens constrain me to glory: Joseph!
  [*He springs up and to her, and takes her into the stable*
ADAM [*in a strong voice*]. His mercy is on them that fear him from
generation to generation.
  [*The* CHORUS, *singing, gather about the* TWO KINGS, *as at first*]
FIRST CHORUS. He hath showed strength with his arm;
SECOND CHORUS. he hath scattered the proud in the imagination
of their hearts.
FIRST CHORUS. He hath put down the mighty from their seats;
SECOND CHORUS. and exalted them of low degree.
FIRST CHORUS. He hath filled the hungry with good things;
SECOND CHORUS. and the rich he hath sent empty away.
THIRD KING [*stretching out his hand towards the* CHORUS]. Are you
now so gay?
  [*As his hand sinks down, they fall on their knees*
And you, lord Adam,
do not speak too soon; you desired the boon of salvation—
have it! You desired twice—me and not me,
the turn and the Return; the Return is here,
take care that you do not now prefer me.
JOSEPH [*coming from the stable*]. Sir, send a midwife to your
daughter.

SEED OF ADAM

All things are rigid; only Mary and I
move, and the glory lies even between us.
The Return is at point to issue; befriend salvation.
      [*All the figures are rigid, except* JOSEPH *and the* THIRD
      KING. ADAM *speaks with difficulty and without moving*]
ADAM. Whom shall I send? whom?
THIRD KING. We, call we you father, are not yours;
we are the things thought of before you, brought
into Eden while men were not, when
in the Days hunger was created, and lives
with a need always to feed on each other. This
was felt in the first kiss of man and woman.
Mother, there is a good cake for you now
to take everlastingly; go, kiss her, love
hungers: deliver her and she shall deliver you.
                [*The* NEGRESS *leaps up and turns on him*
The eaten are on your left hand, the uneaten on your right;
go—there is no thing living so dextrous as you.
                [*The* NEGRESS *and* JOSEPH *go into the stable*
THE ARCHANGEL. Adonai hu ha-elohim!
THIRD KING. What do you see, man? but I see.
Flesh is become that firmament of terrible crystal
your prophet saw: within it wreathed amber
and fire sheathed in the amber; now
the fire and the amber and the crystal are mingled into form;
what do you hear, man? [*He pauses*] but I hear
the terrible sound of the crystal singing as it spins
round the amber where the fire is hidden, and now the amber
is hidden in the crystal, and the crystal spinning into flesh,
twining into flesh: it slows, it stops, it sinks—
what do you know, man? but I know—
it drops into the stretched hands of my mother;
my mother has fetched a child from the womb of its mother;

SEED OF ADAM

my mother has taken the taste of the new bread.
Adonai Elohim!
[JOSEPH *comes from the stable*
JOSEPH. Father Adam, come in; here is your child,
here is the Son of Man, here is Paradise.
To-day everything begins again.
[ADAM *goes down to the door of the stable*
MARY [*meeting him and genuflecting*]. Bless me, father: see how
to-morrow is also now.
ADAM [*making the sign of the Cross*]. Under the Protection!
peace to you, and to all; goodwill to men.
[*They go into the stable*
JOSEPH. Our father Adam is gone in to adore.
THE TSAR. Blessed be he who is the earth's core
THE SULTAN. and splits it all ways with intelligible light.
THE CHORUS. Christ bring us all to the sight
of the pattern of glory which is only he.
THE ARCHANGEL. Yeshua!
THE TSAR. Blessed be he whose intelligence came to save
man from the gripping of the grave: blessed be he.
THE SULTAN. Blessed be he who, because he does all things well,
harries hell by his mercy: blessed be he.
THIRD KING. Blessed be he who is the only Necessity
and his necessity in himself alone.
EVE. Blessed be he who is sown in our flesh, grown
among us for our salvation: blessed be he.
THE CHORUS. Christ bring us, by his clean pact,
into the act which is only he.
THE ARCHANGEL. Yeshua!
THIRD KING. He consumes and is consumed.
THE SULTAN. He is the womb's prophecy and the tomb's.
THE TSAR. He creates, redeems, glorifies: blessed be he.
EVE. He is all our heart finds or lacks.
JOSEPH. He frees our souls from hell's cracks.

THE CHORUS. Christ bring us, by his true birth,
into a new heaven and earth.
JOSEPH. Blessed be he whose love is the knowledge of good
and its motion the willing of good: blessed be he.
THE CHORUS. Adore, adore: blessed for evermore
be the Lord God Sabaoth: blessed be He.

www.ingramcontent.com/pod-product-compliance
Lightning Source LLC
Chambersburg PA
CBHW022129090426
42743CB00008B/1069